Printed in Great Britain
by Amazon

65242525R00058